The Dogs I've Saved

And Other Critters I've Run Into as a Rural Deputy

CHRISTOPHER SJOBLOM

Printed in the United States of America

ISBN Hardcover: 978-1-7343244-6-4
ISBN eBook: 978-1-7343244-5-7

Cover and Interior Design: Creative Publishing Book Design

To all of the organizations and people that fight the good fight to save animals in need.

Introduction

I have been a rural Deputy in Northern Nevada for a little over eight years now. After nearly seven years as a big city cop in Las Vegas, the transition to rural policing was quite significant. I remember talking to one of my old partners in Vegas during my third week on the job up North. "I got into a foot pursuit with two Homicide suspects." He said, "What? I thought it was supposed to be quiet up there." I replied, "Me, too. I just ran down two suspects yesterday, though. A Black Lab and a Chocolate Lab killed four chickens." In an effort to keep this at minimum a PG rated book, I will not print his reply.

As a rural Deputy, I find myself wearing many more hats than I ever could have imagined. One of which is Animal Control when our one official Animal Control is off-duty. In this capacity, I have had the opportunity to catch many dogs that very well could have been injured or killed by speeding motorists, coyotes, mountain lions and to my surprise, porcupines. You will meet Porky and Pine in a little bit. First you get to meet my crew, all of which are rescues. I hope you have as much fun reading this as I did putting it together. Enjoy.

Mike Itty (Say his first and last name really fast and you get My Kitty) is our 14-year-old tabby. He is a recovering Methamphetamine addict. His previous owner used to blow smoke in his face when he was getting high. Mike took two years to recover his Dopamine, but he has turned out to be the coolest cat I've ever had.

These are my girls. Left to right is
Veronica, my German Shepherd,
Hixie, my Black Lab, Ruby, my Bluetick
Coonhound and River, my Border
Collie-Lab-Pitbull mix. Smartest dog
I have ever had. All are rescues.

I called her 'The Wiggla.' She was wagging so hard I thought she might break in half. That and the big Pittie smile made my heart melt. She was happy to jump into my Patrol Vehicle to go for a ride.

Not to be outdone, this Pittie self-served himself right into the shotgun position of my vehicle. I usually transport them in the prisoner compartment, but hey, sometimes you have to be flexible in law enforcement and roll with things as they unfold.

Chipmunk Butt! I was using a motion sensor camera on a theft investigation. I didn't get the thieves on camera, but I got a couple of critters….

2016-08-01 5:29:57 AM   M 1/1
65°F

Critter number 2. A young Jack Rabbit investigating what I suppose is my smell from handling the camera.

Looks like a Border Collie had
date night with a coyote!

I called these two the "Drowsy Duo."
These pathetic puppies didn't even get
up to greet me as I approached the
front door of the residence. Lazy Butts!

I am also a Field Training Officer. I took this picture for the rookies I train. This is so obviously a cop trap that I didn't fall for! This was CLEARLY an ambush set up… Duh, Cops…. Donuts… I snapped the picture for training purposes and got the heck out of there.

I love this guy's beard!

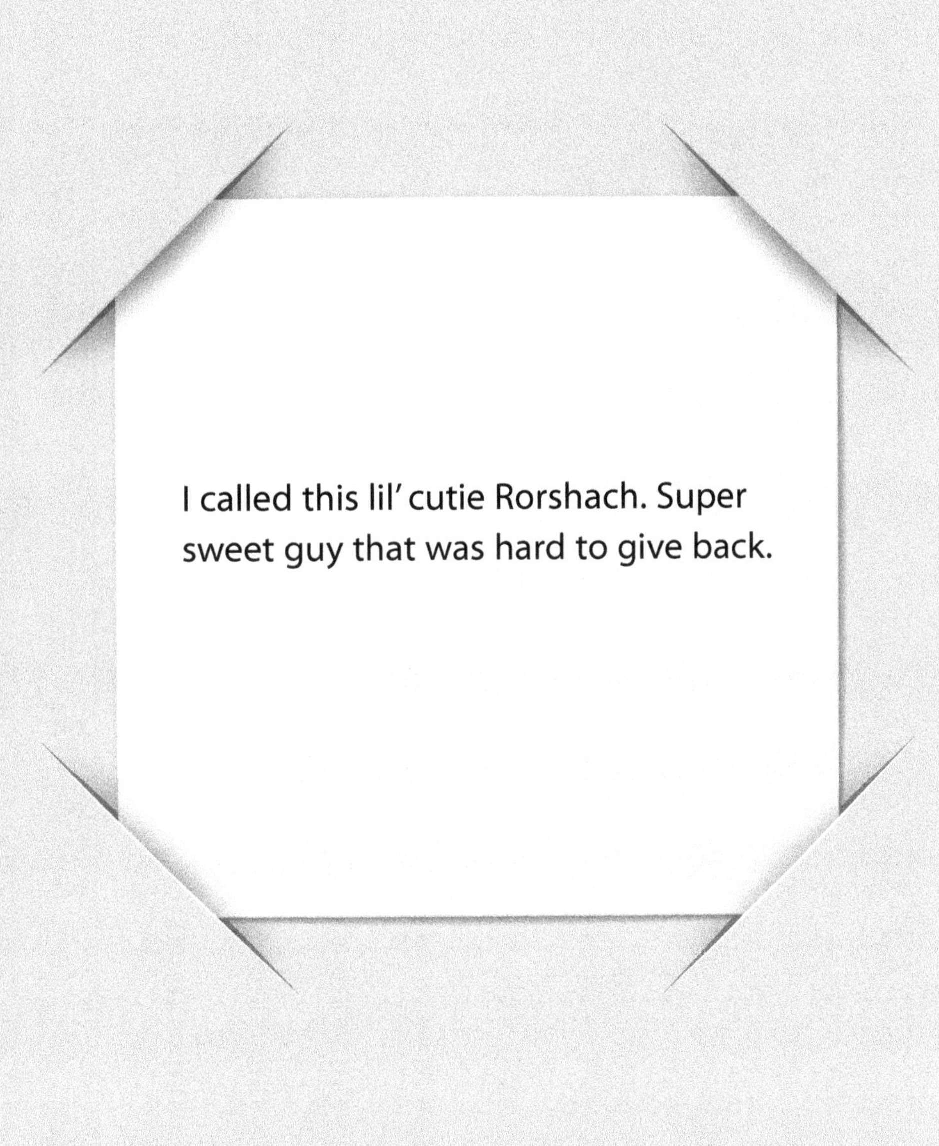

I called this lil' cutie Rorshach. Super sweet guy that was hard to give back.

Unbeknownst to me, this dude actually lives in the yard behind him. When I got out of my rig, the stinker vaulted the four foot chain link fence. He knows the deal and beat me at my game.

Not a dog at large, just a greeter
that was too cute to pass up.

My wife says I love my 'Pointies,'
meaning dogs with pointy ears. I have
had a husky and, of course, Veronica.
Pointies have attitude and these two
Corgis were no exception.

I DO NOT spoil my dogs.
Whatever gave you that idea?

My wife taking a shot at it.

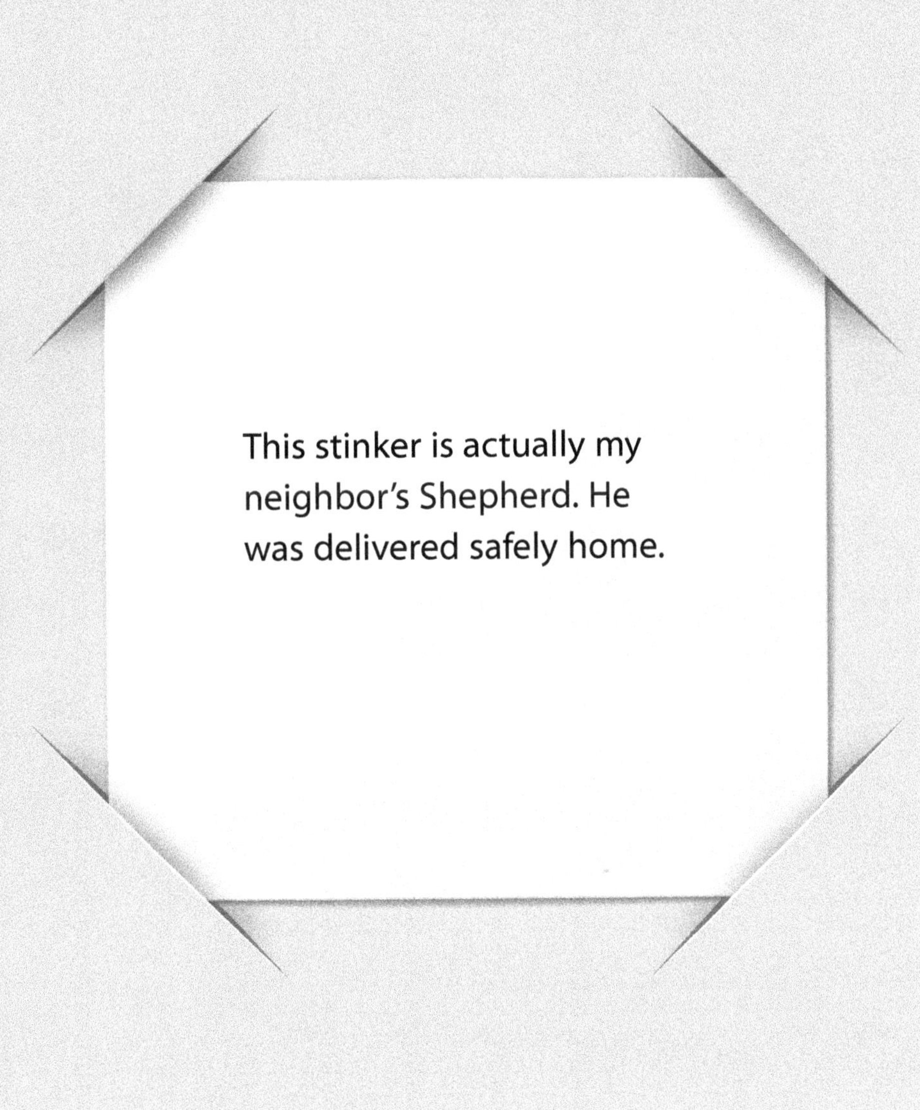
This stinker is actually my
neighbor's Shepherd. He
was delivered safely home.

I swear this was River's sister.

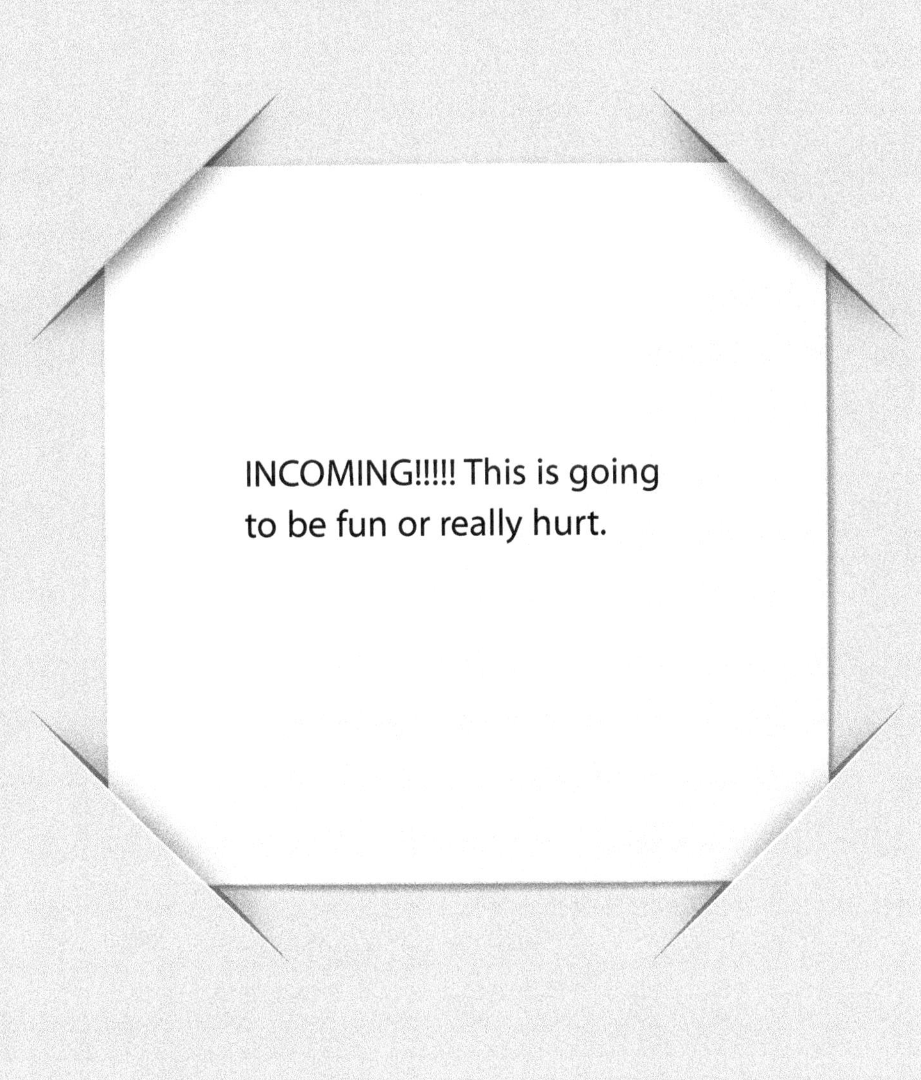

INCOMING!!!!! This is going
to be fun or really hurt.

Whew! I only got body-checked and she ran away. I was happy to avoid becoming a human squeaky toy.

Not sure if this dude was
a mini-Bulldog or just the
runt of the litter.

Warning

The next three pages are a little graphic. Two dogs tangled with a porcupine and lost. If you want to skip past these pictures, jump ahead four pages.

This is the heart-wrenching story of Porky and Pine. I was dispatched to two emaciated dogs that obviously tried to eat a porcupine. This is Porky.

This is Pine. Pine was a little skittish and it took me about twenty minutes to build up trust. I finally got him in my rig and called the emergency vet line to call out a vet on a Saturday.

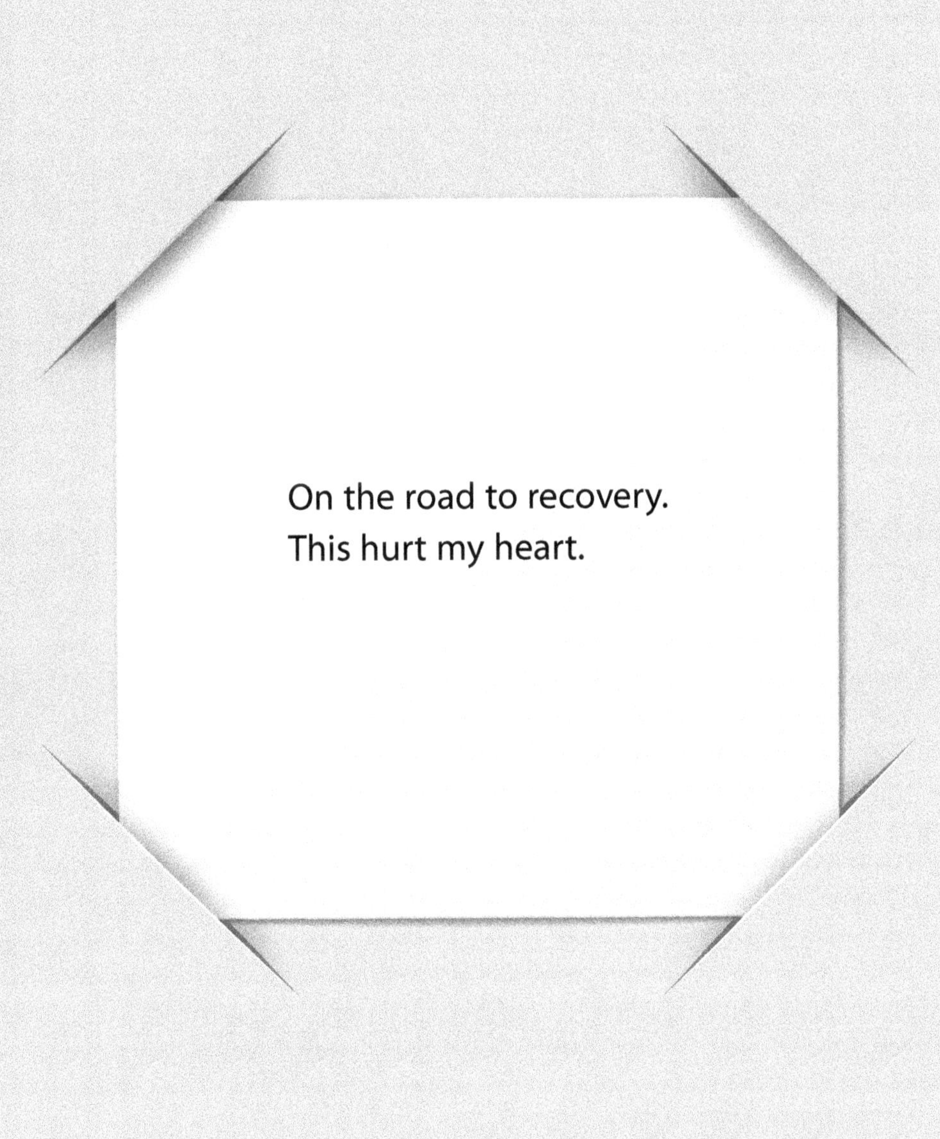
On the road to recovery.
This hurt my heart.

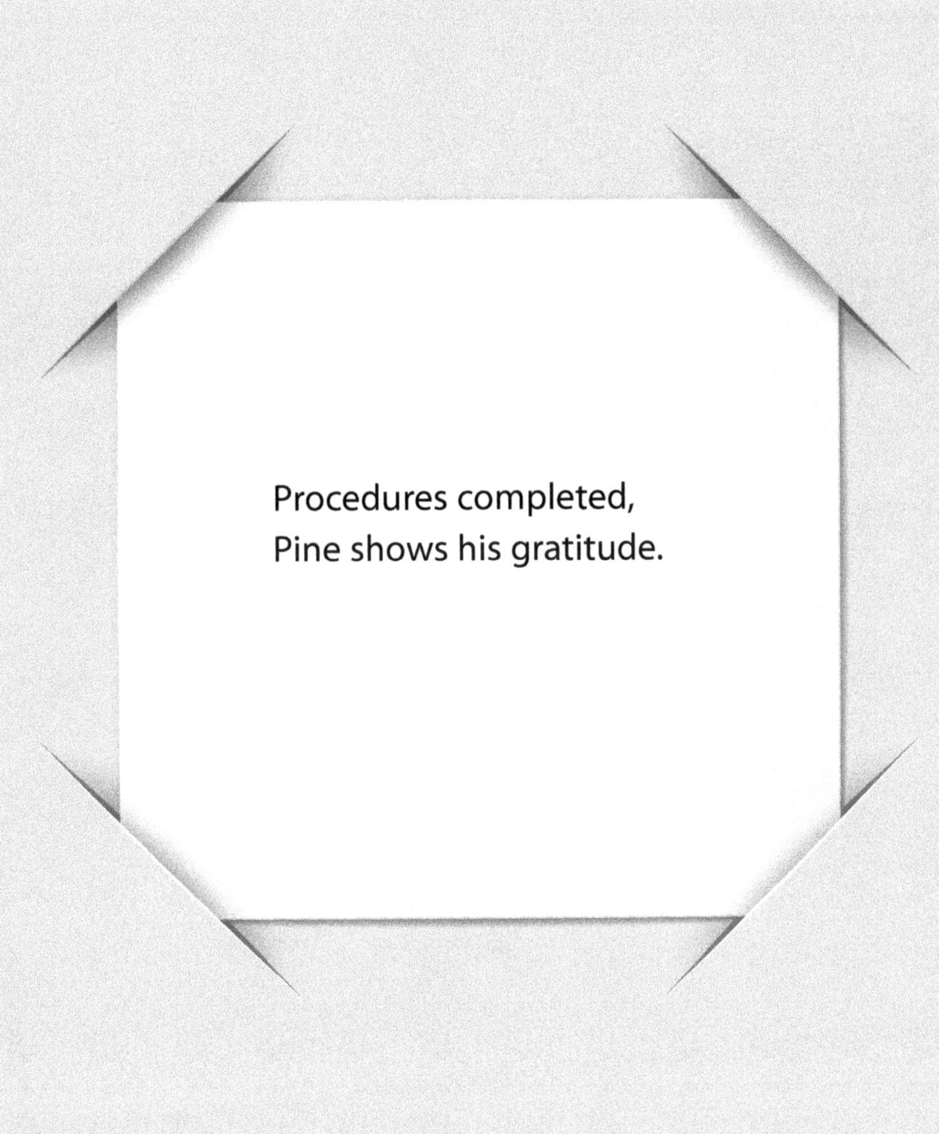

Procedures completed,
Pine shows his gratitude.

Porky and Pine building
up their strength.

Porky expresses her gratitude.

I wound up $480 out of pocket with the vet bill for these two. I would do it again in a heartbeat. A Reno rescue organization picked them up and they found a forever home together. Talk about a happy ending!

Thank you for going through my journey as an amateur dog catcher with me. Look for book two!